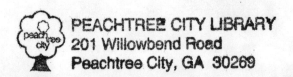

A ROOKIE BIOGRAPHY

JOHN MUIR

Man of the Wild Places

By Carol Greene

CHILDRENS PRESS®
CHICAGO

This book is for Nadine Butcher.

John Muir (1838-1914)

Library of Congress Cataloging-in-Publication Data

Greene, Carol.
John Muir : man of the wild places / by Carol Greene.
    p.   cm. — (A Rookie biography)
Includes index.
Summary: A biography of the naturalist who was an early proponent of
wilderness preservation and helped start the Sierra Club.
ISBN 0-516-04220-3
1. Muir, John, 1838-1914—Juvenile literature. 2. Naturalists—United
States——Juvenile literature. 3. Conservationists—United States—
Juvenile literature. [1. Muir, John, 1838-1914. 2. Naturalists
3. Conservationists..] I. Title. II. Series: Greene, Carol. Rookie biography.
QH31.M9G68   1991
508.794′092—dc20
[B]
[92]   90-19993
                                                CIP
                                                AC

John Muir was a real person.
He was born in 1838.
He died in 1914.
John Muir loved nature
and the wild places.
He worked to save them.
This is his story.

TABLE OF CONTENTS

Chapter 1

A Boy in Scotland

John heard a noise.
He jumped up.
His grandfather said
it was just the wind.
But John wanted to find out
what was making the noise.

At last he dug in the haystack.
There he found the noise-makers
—a mouse and her babies.

"That was a wonderful
discovery to me," said John.

He was only three.
But he had found
something important.
He had found nature.

John Muir's family
lived in Dunbar, Scotland.
John's father was strict.
He beat John.
So did John's teacher.
Both men thought beatings
helped children learn.

John Muir's
home in Dunbar,
Scotland

John and his friends
fought each other.
They wanted to be
soldiers someday.
So John was often sore.
But he had good times too.

At night he and his brother
David played "scootchers."
It was a game of dares.
They dared each other
to climb things or to go
into a spooky room.

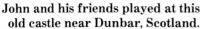
John and his friends played at this
old castle near Dunbar, Scotland.

Sometimes John played
with his friends
at an old castle.

Sometimes they swam
in little sea pools.
They always poked sticks
into the pools first.
A boy-eating monster
might live at the bottom.

Most of all, they loved
to run through the hills.
They ran past farms.
They ran through woods.
They ran in wind and rain.
They could run 20 miles.

John knew his father
would beat him later.
But he didn't care.

"We were free," he said.

Chapter 2

Farm Boy

When John was 11,
his family moved
to the United States of America.
They lived on a farm in Wisconsin.

At first John was happy.
He loved the trees and birds,
the flowers and frogs,
and the lightning bugs.
He even loved the storms.

In Wisconsin, John
explored the woods
and streams (opposite).
He studied
wildflowers (above)
and birds such as
owls (left).

House on the Muir farm near Portage, Wisconsin

But soon John's father
put him to work.
They were farmers now.
John must clear land,
plow, hoe, harvest,
and build fences.

John worked on that farm
for eight long years.
He worked even
when he was sick.

Then his father
bought a new farm.
John had to start
all over again.

Nature helped John get
through the hard times.
When he was cold,
he watched the birds.
When he was tired,
he studied tree roots.

**Farmland in
Wisconsin**

John liked taking walks by this lake.

Friends helped him too.
They cheered him up
and lent him books.
John liked math, poems,
and books about travel.

John's friends said
he should leave the farm.
But John waited.
Then, when he was 22,
he packed a sack and left.

Chapter 3

A Dream

John took a train
to Madison, Wisconsin.
People were kind to him.
They helped him get jobs
and study at the university.

The University of Wisconsin at Madison

One day, a friend talked
to John about plants.
John had always loved plants.
Now he wanted to study them.

Soon he had a dream.
Wouldn't it be grand
to spend his life
learning about nature
in America's wild places?

A lake in the Canadian Rockies, Alberta, Canada

In 1864, John went
to Canada for a while.
He traveled around
and collected plants.
This *was* the life for him.

But John had to work.
He was good with machines.
So he spent some time
working in factories.

One day, when he was
fixing a machine,
he hurt his eye.
Soon he couldn't see at all.

John Muir

The doctor said John
would see again.
But John didn't want
to see any more factories.
He wanted to see nature.

So John decided to walk
all the way to South America.
He left in 1867.
He saw a lot of nature
—trees, mountains, swamps,
Spanish moss, and alligators.

As he went along,
John wrote in his journal.

John Muir discovered many wonders
as he journeyed through South America,
including alligators (top left), waterfalls
(top right), great mountains (bottom left),
high-altitude farms (bottom right), and
flowers by the side of the road (center).

He wrote that all
the little pieces of nature
work together perfectly.
He wrote that God
loves everything in the world,
not just people.

John went as far as Cuba.
Then he got sick.
But he knew where
he wanted to go next
—to California.

John Muir visited Cuba's
lush tropical forests

Chapter 4

The Wild Places

Many people went to
California to make money.
John Muir went
to find the wild places.
And he did.

**John explored
California's
wild places.**

The California poppy is a wildflower that grows in grassy meadows.

He found a valley
that looked like
"a sheet of flowers."
He found the beautiful
Sierra Nevada mountains.
He wanted to stay forever.

So John became a shepherd.
In the summer, he took
his sheep into the mountains.
But John wanted to go
where tame sheep couldn't go.

The high Sierra Nevada mountains are
in the eastern part of California.

The beautiful Yosemite Valley (above) lies about two hundred miles east of San Francisco. Yosemite Falls (opposite page) in Yosemite National Park

So he began to work
part-time for a hotel.
He spent the rest of
his time in the mountains.
Soon the Yosemite Valley
became his real home.

John didn't need much.
He ate bread and oatmeal.
He drank tea and water.
He made his bed from
the branches of fir trees.

John didn't hunt.
He hated to kill things.
But he studied everything
—ants, bears, grasshoppers,
flowers, trees, birds,
raindrops, and glaciers.

Redwood trees (opposite page) in Muir Woods
National Monument near San Francisco,
California. John Muir (below) examines spots in
petrified wood on a trip to Alaska.

John saw life
in everything,
even in rocks
and water.

"What wonders
lie in every
mountain day!"
he wrote.

John's friend, Jeanne Carr,
said he should publish
what he wrote about nature.
At last John did.

Now he had to leave
the mountains sometimes.
John didn't like that.
But his writing helped others
love the wild places too.

In 1880, John married
a woman called Louie.
Louie was special.
She knew John must spend
time in the wild places.

This photograph of John and Louie Muir was
taken in the later years of their marriage.

Muir Glacier in Alaska was discovered by John Muir in 1879.

So John went to Alaska.
There he explored a glacier.
A little black dog called
Stickeen went with him.
They stayed all day.

Then snow began to fall.
The wind blew hard.
They came to a crack in the ice.
It was 50 feet wide.
A thin ice bridge crossed it.

John was afraid, but
somehow he got over.
But Stickeen seemed to cry,
"No-o-o, I can never go-o-o . . ."

The face of a glacier and the Stickeen River, named after Muir's dog

John kept calling him
and calling him.
At last, inch by inch,
Stickeen crept across the ice.
Then he raced all over.
He seemed to yell,
"Saved! Saved! Saved!"

John wrote about Stickeen.
He never forgot that brave dog.

John Muir's daughters

Before long, John and Louie
had two little girls.
Then John felt he must
earn more money.

Louie's family had
a fruit farm.
John ran it and
made a lot of money.
But he wasn't happy.

John Muir with his wife and daughters in 1901

Louie saw that.
So she made John go
back to the wild places.
She said he must
do his real work.
She was right.

Chapter 5

Battles

Writing about
nature was
hard work
for John.
He said it
made his head
hot, his feet
cold, and his
stomach restless.

Muir's writings made
many people aware
of the need to
conserve our
natural resources.

Cutting all the trees in a forest is bad for the land.
The wind and rain carry the precious soil away.

But John knew people
were doing bad things
to the wild places.
They chopped down trees.
They let tame animals—
cattle and sheep—
graze in wild valleys.

John used his writing
to fight for wild places.
"People need beauty
as well as bread," he wrote.

John Muir stands beside a huge redwood tree in Muir Woods.

John Muir with a Sierra Club group on the trail to Hetch Hetchy Valley

Others felt that way too.
John worked with them.
In 1890, they got
the government to make
Yosemite a national park.

In 1892, John and his friends
started the Sierra Club.
It watches over wild places
and helps people enjoy them.
John was its first president.

By now, John was famous.
He traveled all over.
He met other famous people.
In 1903, he took
the president of the United States,
Theodore Roosevelt,
camping in Yosemite.

John Muir (right) persuaded President Theodore Roosevelt
(left) to set aside 148 million acres of forest preserves.

Theodore Roosevelt (center) worked with John Muir (fourth from right)
to protect the California redwood forest

President Roosevelt loved
the wild places too.
He said he would help
John fight for them.

In 1905, Louie Muir died.
John missed her.
But he went on fighting
for the wild places.
He won more battles.
He lost some too.

He wanted to save
the Hetch Hetchy Valley.
But the government let
people build a dam there.
John said that was
"hard to bear."

The dam at Hetch Hetchy supplies power and water to
San Francisco, but the valley that Muir tried to save
disappeared under the lake that the dam created.

The moon rising over Yosemite
Valley (top). A stamp (bottom)
was issued to commemorate
the work of John Muir.

When John was 76,
he became very ill.
But he wasn't afraid.

He said all things die.
But God watches over them.
Death was like going home
to bed in the evening.
He would get up again
in the morning.

During his last years, John Muir continued to write
and to visit his beloved Yosemite Valley.

John Muir died
on Christmas Eve, 1914.

Important Dates

1838   April 21—Born in Dunbar, Scotland, to Daniel and Anne Muir

1849   Moved with family to Wisconsin

1868   Went to California

1880   Married Louie Strentzel
Explored Taylor Glacier with Stickeen

1890   Yosemite made a national park

1892   Helped start Sierra Club

1903   Camped with President Theodore Roosevelt

1914   December 24—Died in Los Angeles, California

INDEX

Page numbers in boldface type indicate illustrations.

PHOTO CREDITS

ABOUT THE AUTHOR

Carol Greene has degrees in English literature and musicology. She has worked
in international exchange programs, as an editor, and as a teacher. She now
lives in St. Louis, Missouri, and writes full-time. She has published more than
eighty books. Others in the Rookie Biographies series include *Hans Christian
Andersen, Ludwig van Beethoven, Black Elk, Elizabeth Blackwell, Daniel Boone,
Christopher Columbus, Jacques Cousteau, Elizabeth the First, Benjamin
Franklin, Martin Luther King, Jr., Robert E. Lee, Abraham Lincoln, Louis
Pasteur, Pocahontas, Jackie Robinson, George Washington,* and *Laura Ingalls
Wilder.*